SEEKING SOLACE

What Autistic People Really Think and Feel

Seeking Solace with Sammy and Friends

Copyright © 2018

Cover & illustrations by: Catina Burkett

Email: she2autism@yahoo.com

Website: www.She2autism.com

I love to read and research tree house collections from around the world. No one around me likes to do these things so I play alone.

Hello my name is Sammy. People call me Sammy *Same Same* because I like doing the same thing every day. I'm happy. I want other people to be happy too. My mom says I should do things with other people so that we can be happy together.

Mom says other people feel left out and I don't understand why? I have mom, dad and a swell group of friends to help me figure it all out. Maybe they can help you too. So come on. Meet my family and friends.

Hi, I'm dad. I love Sammy so much. Most of the time he seem to be in a world of his own. I show Sammy the fun things I did when I was a kid but it does not interest Sammy.
DAD

He doesn't play basket, baseball or soccer with the other kids. It's a great way to make friends. Sometimes I don't understand and I often wish Sammy could fit in and have friends too. This makes me feel sad.

Hi, I'm mom. There are so many great things about Sammy. He is honest, does not pick on others, loves to read and play with his train set for hours at a time. Sammy does not like loud noise, he's quiet, creative and kind but It's hard for Sammy to make friends. I want him to have fun and enjoy all the things that everyone else loves and do.

Boutique
MOM

I worry that he spends so much time alone and he gets frustrated in groups of kids his age. Sometimes I cry because I feel sad watching Sammy struggle to get along with others.

Everyday I have to do what others want but they don't have to do things that I like. I rather be alone.

Hi I'm Tavis. I try to socialize like everyone else but I get so tired and sometimes noise wears me out .
My family likes to play music and dance. I love music too. Just not too often or too long!

HOUSE PARTY !!

I dream of running away

Hello my name is Sergeant Lyles. Sammy's neighbor. I retired from the military after 20 years. I was injured in battle. I lost an arm and part of my leg. It's been tough adjusting to *normal* life after fighting in war. I often ask myself. What's *normal*?

I have a cabin and a treehouse. Sammy is welcome to visit sometimes.
I love treehouses!

Hello I'm Mr. Russell, Sammy's school counselor. Sammy is a very special kid. We spend much time together. Some people have problems accepting Sammy and his unique personality that makes It hard to make friends. It's like mixing oil and water. For example, Water and oil don't mix.

Sammy has Mild Autism. He is very high functioning so he would be an oil person. We call non-autistic people Water people.

Mild means is harder for Non Autistic people to recognize and accept symptoms because oil and water people look alike but they are made differently.

Sammy is like a sensory bottle. You can mix a bottle of colored water with colored oil. The colors may change for seconds but each color will separate and hold their original color. No matter how much or how hard you shake it together.

People like Sammy are be so beautiful inside, like these sensory bottles. Most people don't get to see how creative and amazing Sammy is.

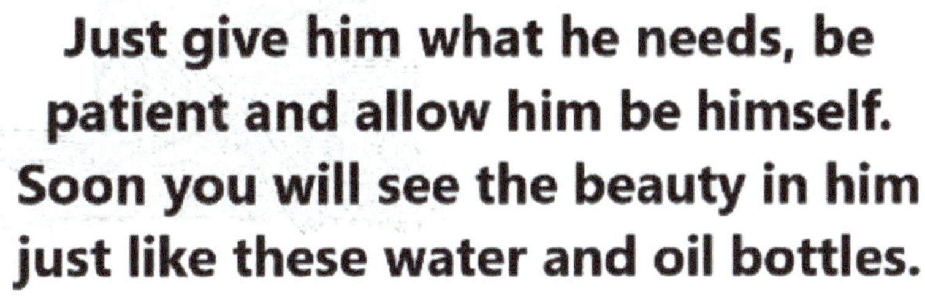

Just give him what he needs, be patient and allow him be himself. Soon you will see the beauty in him just like these water and oil bottles.

Hi, I'm Angel B. and I was an Oil person too until I was called to the sky.

Father Angel lives in Mt. Solace and he sends me all around the world to help oil people and their families communicate in a world of water.

I have two Angel guides. Donny helps guys and Marie helps girls.

Sometimes we pair together to demonstrate how guys and girls should communicate. We also show you what not to do! That is very important!

Our toughest assignments is teaching Sammy and his friend how to deal with Empty Edna and the Bottomless Pitts.
Meet Norman, Judy & Edna aka The Bottomless Pitts

Hi I'm Edna!
I have the newest shoes but I'm not the first to get them. My makeup set is better than Anna's but Rayna has the best I ever seen and I have seen the new movie before it came out. I have nre phone that came out but I want the new computer too.

Im trying to tell you about the fight I saw, the best name brand clothes and how easy it is to lie to the math teacher. Are you listening Sammy?
How does anyone enjoy lying, watching people get hurt and trying to impress others ?

I have the perfect peer mentor to show you how to behave and get along with people. I know you can do this Sammy.
I didn't ask for help. Please stop trying to change me. There's nothing wrong with me.

Ms. Tilly is a very nice teacher who does not know the oil and water relationship in communication. Working together with Angel Guides will help get our message through clearly.
Oil
H_2O

This is conforming Norman. He constantly tells Sammy what to do, how to speak to people, when to speak, what other people are feeling and thinking. He even tells Sammy to stop being quiet.

Why do I have to worry about making people I don't know like me?

Blah, Blah, Blah, Blah
You need to be more
Blah, Blah, Blah, Blah
People won't like you
Blah, Blah, Blah, Blah

This is Judy.
Judy hangs around me. I don't know why because she complains so much. I deal with it because I don't have many friends.
Sammy's cool but sometimes I don't think he likes me. I don't think he likes people.

Sometimes Judy is not nice to me. She changes so much. It's like she's four different people.

Sad
Judy
Angry
Judy
Drama
Judy

Sammy settles for Judy's company because he doesn't like to be alone all the time.
Your boring Sammy. Be more spontaneous !
You don't care how I feel.
Your not my real friend.

My facial expression usually stays the same. People say I don't care but I feel all of the same emotions they do. I feel it very deep but it doesn't always show on my face.

I need time alone when I feel all those feelings. I get very tired too.

sammy's need for sleep and rest will be demonstrated with using a glass of water.
PEOPLE LIKE SAMMY
FULL CUP
ALMOST EMPTY
WATER PEOPLE

Overflow is dangerous to Oil people. Many call it over stimulation.
This cup overflows with water. Water people see this as a blessing of having more than enough.
OVERFLOW
FULL CUP

Water people, easily mix and blend. This pitcher is filled with different emotions all mixed together. Mixing all these emotions together can cause change.

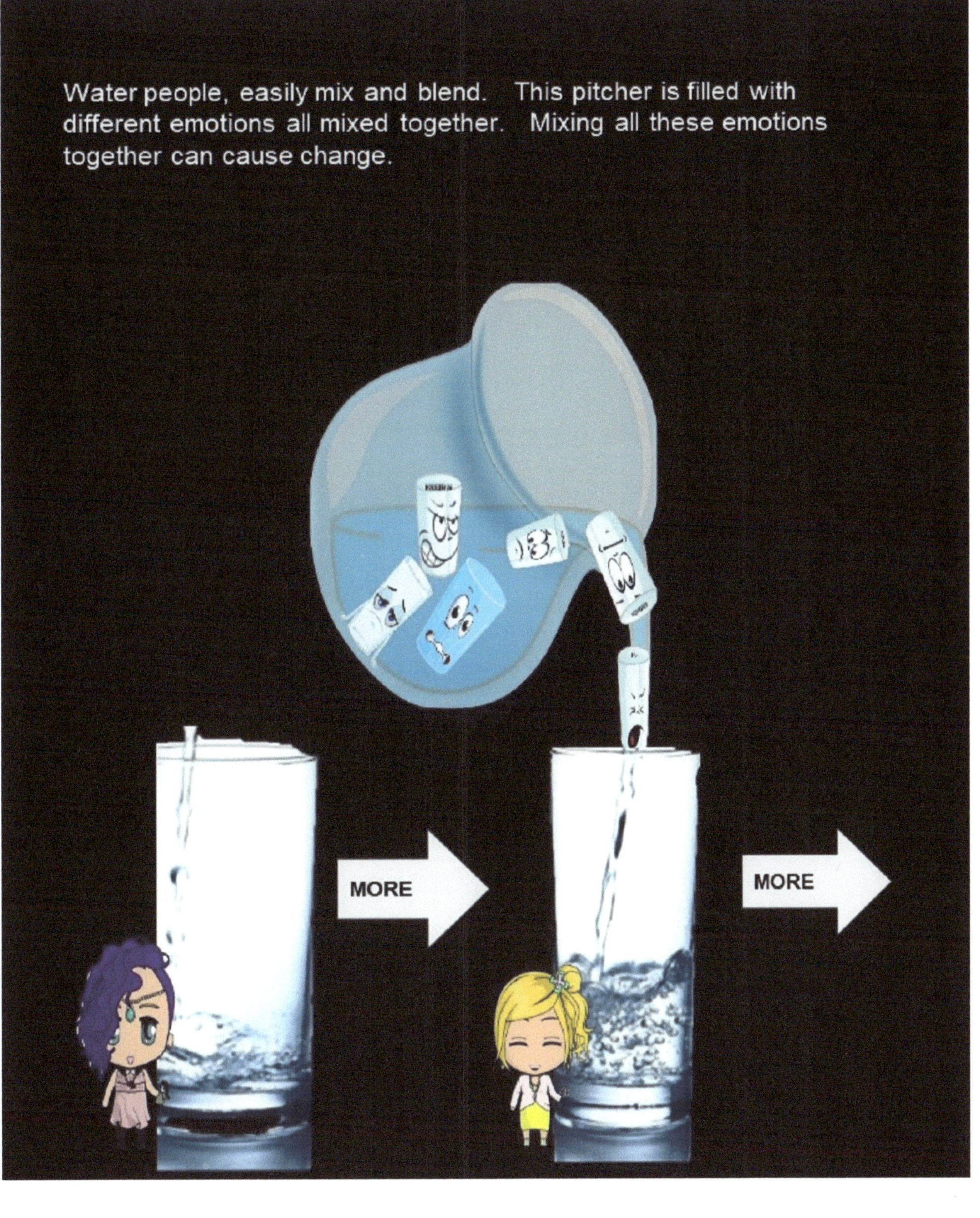

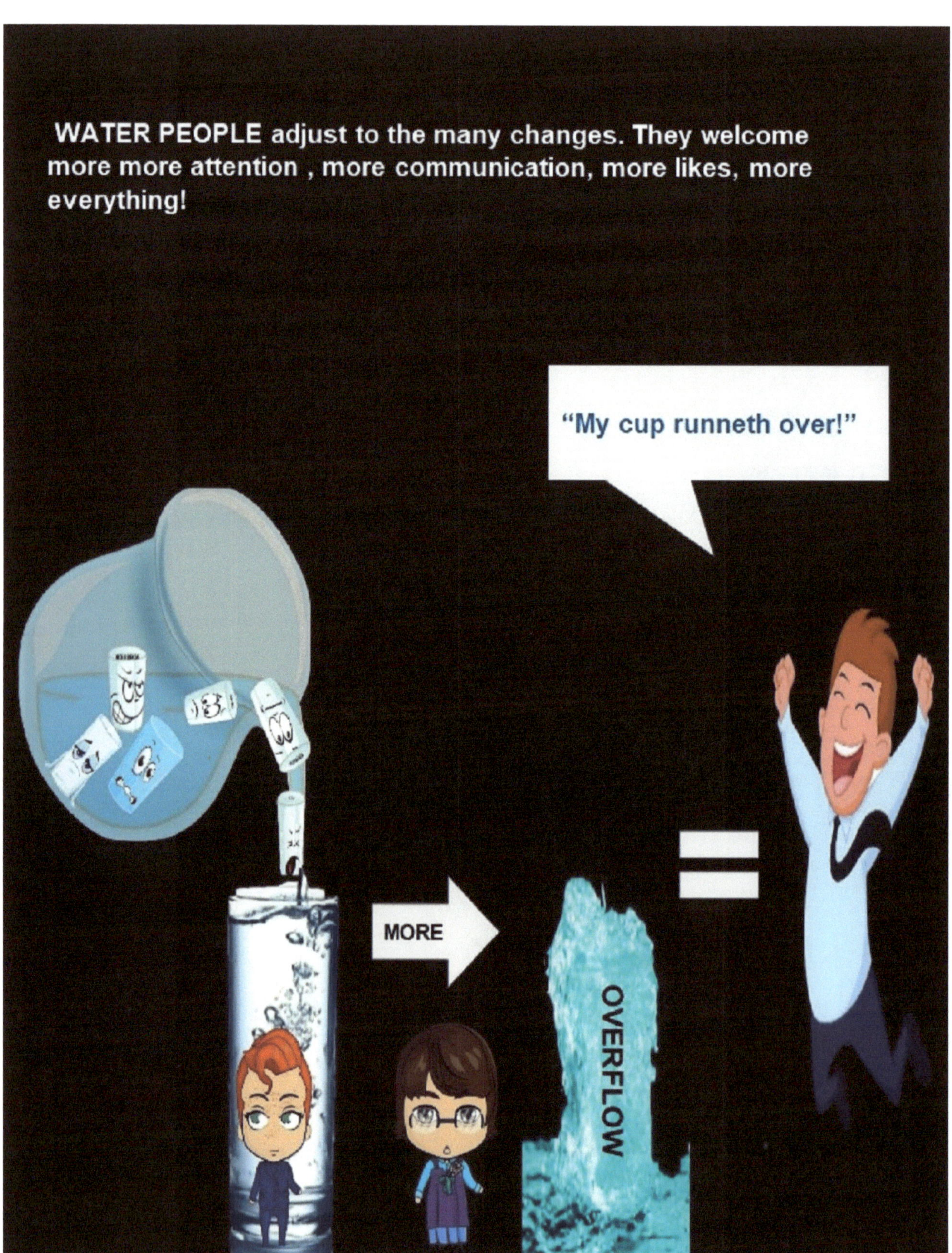

WATER PEOPLE adjust to the many changes. They welcome more more attention , more communication, more likes, more everything!
"My cup runneth over!"
MORE
OVERFLOW
=

Oil people work very hard to keep their cup full by not changing too much. Blending and mixing is very difficult.
Oil people try to manage all the attention and changes but it's very overwhelming.

An overflow of **WATER PEOPLES** attention, changes, needs, noise and emotions is overwhelming and devastating to Oil people.

People tell me im rude because I don't smile.
I see other people smile while being mean. It's not right.   It's confusing.

Sammy's cup of is full with trying to communicate his thoughts, feelings and doing the right thing. Everyday is filled with watching people do things he doesn't emotionally understand.

Somedays Sammy stays in his room and sleeps for hours and hours.
ZZzzz
zzz

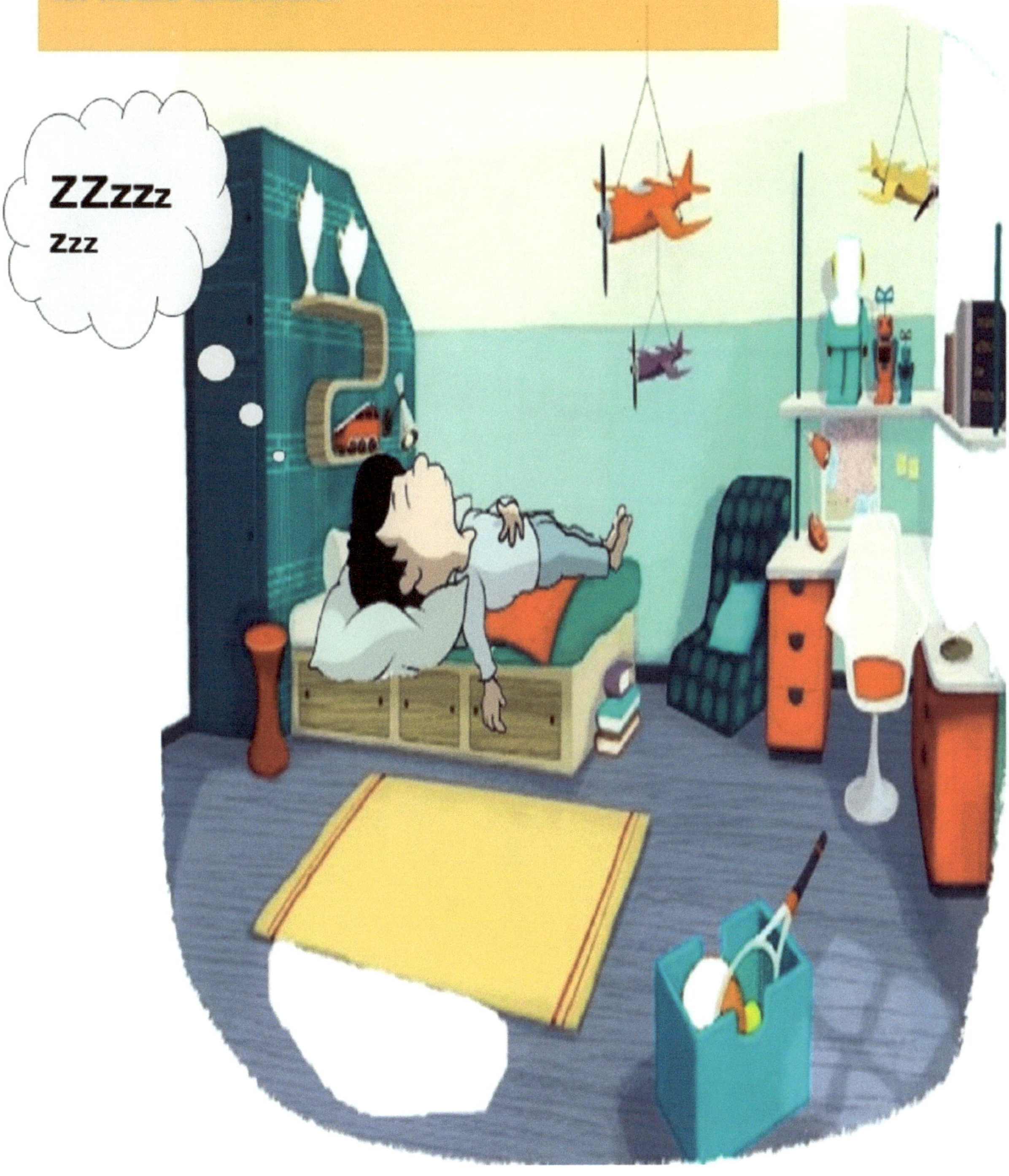

Tavis and Sammy dream of getting away to the land of Solace.

THE END

Sammy same same and his friend Tavis are young boys with mild autism. They have significant social problems with communication. Sammy is nicknamed *same same* because change is difficult. Tavis is called Tired Tavis because he is often overwhelmed with noise, crowds and being off schedule. This book is a series told from the viewpoint of Sammy and Tavis. Readers get insight into their thinking, feelings, behaviors and why they respond to the environment in the way that they do. What makes this book special is that it is written by a licensed mental health professional that has mild autism. For the first time readers get to learn about the confusion and frustration from both sides. This book introduces a world called Solace that Sammy and Tavis wish existed. There are Angels that guide Sammy, Tavis, family, friends and caretakers. These Angels had mild autism when they were mortals on earth. The Angels introduce the world of Solace to the characters. On Solace, the boys are wanted ,liked and accepted. Solace is a place that that is magical and comforting. One of the first lessons is knowing the difference between the two types of people in the world. Oil people and Water people. People like Sammy and Tavis are Oil and everyone else is Water. Everyone knows that oil and water don't mix but with understanding, planning and positive intentions, water and oil can create something beautiful that benefits everyone. This book has adventure and life lessons for all ages.

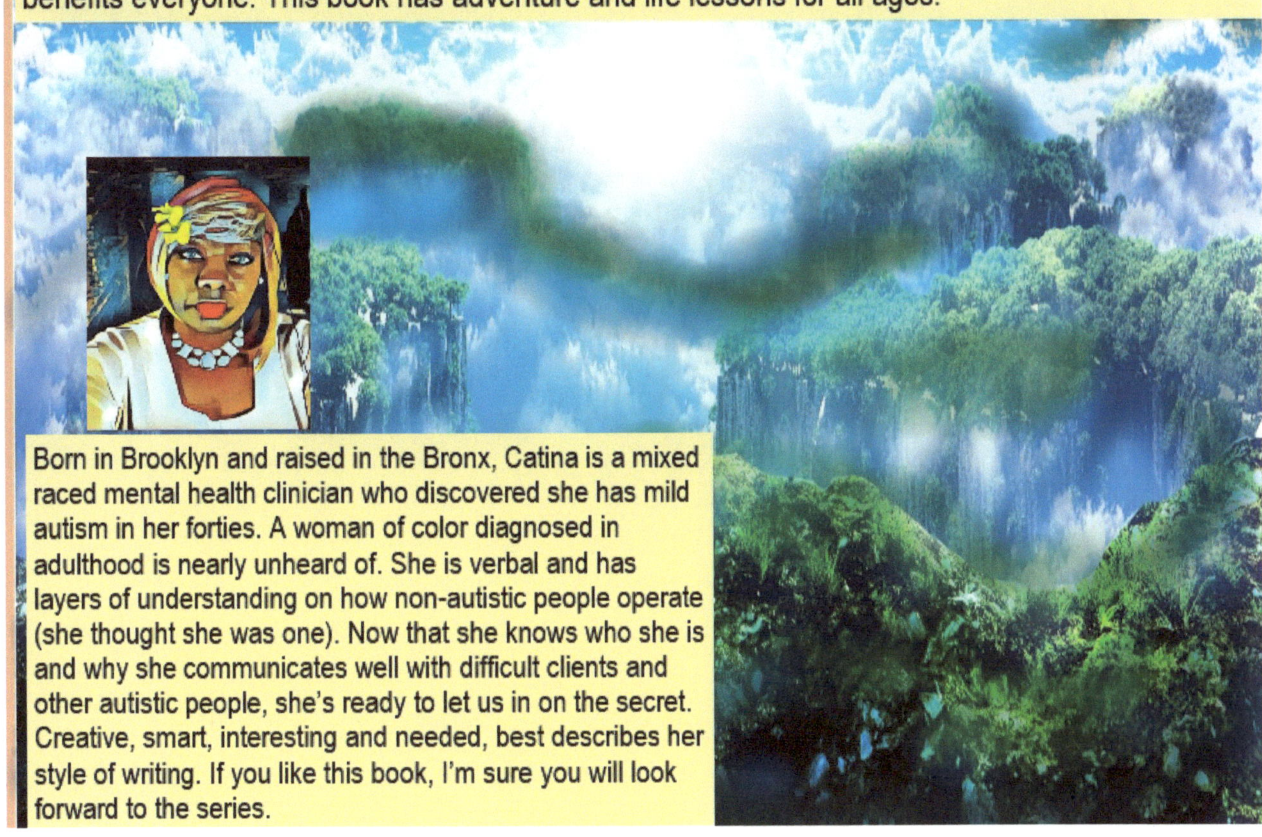

Born in Brooklyn and raised in the Bronx, Catina is a mixed raced mental health clinician who discovered she has mild autism in her forties. A woman of color diagnosed in adulthood is nearly unheard of. She is verbal and has layers of understanding on how non-autistic people operate (she thought she was one). Now that she knows who she is and why she communicates well with difficult clients and other autistic people, she's ready to let us in on the secret. Creative, smart, interesting and needed, best describes her style of writing. If you like this book, I'm sure you will look forward to the series.